Stones Ripe for Sowing

STONES RIPE FOR SOWING

Poems

Libby Bernardin

Press 53
Winston-Salem

Press 53, LLC
PO Box 30314
Winston-Salem, NC 27130

First Edition

Cover design by Kevin Morgan Watson

Cover art, "Stacked Stones," Copyright © 2017
by Philip Wilkinson, used by permission of the artist.

Author photo by Philip Wilkinson

Library of Congress Control Number
2018949964

Printed on acid-free paper
ISBN 978-1-941209-85-1

to my sister, Ellen

and in memory of our brother Bub and our sister Garnet

Live in my absence as if in a house.
Absence is a house so vast
        that inside you will pass through its walls
        and hang pictures on the air.
                                —Pablo Neruda

Grateful acknowledgment is made to the editors of the journals and anthologies who first published the following poems, sometimes in an earlier version.

Asheville Poetry Review: "Meteor Shower"

Cairn 43: "Solstice"

Cairn 49: "Transubstantiation"

Fall Lines Literary Magazine: "Easing Westward"

A Gathering of Poets 2016 (Anthology): "From East Coast to West"

Jasper Magazine: "As if I Blinked"

Kakalak 2016: "I found the photograph after" (honorable mention)

The New Review: "Plum Blossoms"

Pinesong (North Carolina Poetry Society): "Among Stones" (First Place in Poetry of Courage Award,) "Transmigration" (First Place in Poetry of Witness Award)

Poetry Society of South Carolina: "Naming in the Garden at the Headwaters of the Tigris and the Euphrates," "*And when the forest of your bearable life appears*," and "Like Wings"

The World Is Charged: Poetic Engagements with Gerard Manley Hopkins (Anthology): "And the Great White Pelicans"

Contents

A Letter to Susan, in Ireland

Dear You,

there in Kylemoor Gardens among nasturtiums,
rows of sedum, and flowering Kale, all twisting
in aimless route down the brick wall, like vegetables
stretching through rows and rows in a far field.

You among gorse growing on the craggy shore, brash
among the *squelch and slap* of *soggy peat* lured by sea's
swoosh of waves, or among heather one might look
longingly at from a window, as I do at bulrush in my briny marsh.

Is that Sweet-grass wind-waving on lily pad shore
its loose inflorescence like pink feathers? I read
that *Spartina* has invaded the bogs where you are,
so far away in the Celtic land of lilt and Hawthorne lyric.

Here it has rained all day, a welcome relief. The eclipse
will occur on August 21 @ 1:22 p.m.—or maybe it's 2 p.m.—
Anyway, I will watch from the bay. I don't know if the Irish
will see moon shadow sun, so you may miss it, the darkness here—

You, *when your breath plumes in the frost* in winter,
and you need to get in touch from Galway, turn toward
the most familiar flowers in low country gardens—
say marigolds, zinnias or geraniums.

I haven't hawthorn but the camellia near my house—
the one I call Flame Azalea on the corner, away from my porch
holds the light well, especially in early morn.

> —in memory of Susan Laughter Meyers
> (1945 – 2017)

I

Black-Eyed Susan

Like Queen Esther,
  she does not refuse
her duty, her fair face
  leans into sun,
unflinching,
  even at noon's parching.
Her dark eye blackens
  at fierce heat,
roots thrive in dry soil—
  She waits,
assured of a place
  among her tribe—
her grace finds favor,
  and though bloom
withers, she braves
  wind, scattering seeds
like grain cast
  among the famished.

Meteor Shower

We see from earth, space debris like pinpoints,
      chipped from radiant pebbles,
            though their might could smite us closer up.

Does some Ancient Mother
      sweep to clear
            a path for children?

When meteors shower, I see my grandmother
      scattering seed from her apron, feeding
            chickens whose beaks just miss her feet.

She is not thinking of astronomy—or chickens,
      though I saw her gaze lift over the silent
            moonlit pasture one Alabama evening,

her face lit with wonder, feet tapping
      to some inner music she wouldn't—
            or couldn't sing to me.

Here I stand, in the rippling dark,
      yet *untouched, untold, altogether unreached*,
            seeking the god-like immensity of ordinary things.

If I could speak to the god of our childhood

I could rid myself of this anger
I try not to express in the presence of the sacred.
We have been loved and lucky,

with long lives. No regrets,
not even our arguments,
like the time I found my white blouse

crumpled on the floor,
and you replied indifferently,
I needed it, as if it was your privilege.

The god of our childhood
left long ago, so to whom shall I pray
except my dead? Dear Sister,

listen, and put glad thoughts
in my head, direction in my steps,
through all my last winters.

I do this for you,

my younger sister, whom I imagined
        would not pass to the other side before I do—
                but do I want to weep now you're at peace?

I grow my hair silver to remind myself
        I'm no longer young, though don't think
                I haven't tried each day to forget.

As a wild storm blows down a house,
        you and our history are blown—
                maybe into an inlet,

or under the crumbled pier,
        fragile pilings bereft, splintered ends
                trying to scratch the sky.

Wisteria

across my street hanging
low among the plum blossoms

lavender racemes—pendulous
and elegant—pea-like orbs

grouped as though grapes
on a stem

Look at the thick vine
clambering clockwise

up the plum tree trunk
taking over blossoms

shaking in wind: fragility
scattered from velvet pods

into poison seeds
How like us, our true selves

deadened by words,
by anger gusting in wind

Stasis

Night holds sway over the rooster's crowing.
It stills the adrenalin swoosh of those who wake in haste,

and holds the sun at bay from burning away our sleep.
The tintinnabulation of unheard bells anticipates

Advent, and our restless soles gain the floor at last.
We sit bedside to hear light emerge, surround us,

as though a holy dream consecrated the night
and day equally, *sotto voce* articulation of union

beyond the bodies where we linger—thin curtain
separating us from what we don't know—

the cock's cry pierces dawn. We rise with first light
splash our face with cool water and reach, reach—

Solstice

Even in winter one can plant flowers,
patterns of snapdragons, pansies, hollyhocks,

buddleia, one climbing rose, hydrangea,
John's mums, Lizzy's daylilies, Meg's

gold, yellow, and red tulips—
blooming awaits the moon's pull,

Saturn and Jupiter, king of all heaven,
lures Venus, illuminates the wait—

Even in winter, when the earth is still,
we take our lives into our hands,

and step into doubt, that hard stone,
seed of spring, of water, of fire.

Consider the Cardinal

Some say if you see them flying toward sun,
good luck will come to you,
but cardinals stay warm in winter

constantly foraging close to ground,
in shrubs, and grass or at feeders.

In spring, they nest in tangled vines or scrub.
Mated pairs sing their news,

             and so might we
whistle through moss tapestry,
nesting at ease amid possible predators,

with faith in a guarding mate or avian god—
no matter how accessible the nest.

What missal holds the text of our salvation
from any benighted place—or even ephemeral shelter?

Do we, uneasy in old dispensations, flee
from the old ways, take short trips
through thickets, forage in hard and doubtful places?

And the Great White Pelicans

lifted themselves with such grace
that I felt some blessing fall upon us
from the black-tipped wings gathering air,
pulling themselves away from earth
as though a white shawl had shook itself
then folding back in the wind, took our breath
from us with long orange-yellow beaks
then circled back on Marsh Island
on ocean shore, sand, grass
black feel gathered into some
300-count of white plumage—
magnificent restless stalking,
we unwilling to leave what we were given
so that turning away, our hearts stirred
by the splendor of a thing,
I stared longingly over our wake,
nothing illusory in the parting white foam,
nothing unreal in the beating wings.

She Who Listens to Hummingbirds

This guttural breath of thunder
   commands me to find her, feet
planted in snow far from home—
   hands beckoning from her curtain
of raven hair, face smooth as river
   pearls, her skirt purple hyacinth.
We sit and watch whatever
   these shivery trees are, as her hair
turns silver, then on my knees,
   right hand trembling with one
wild stream of hair, my left
   gathering another, I braid to her waist—
Spirit, let wind stir though it empties
   my hands of her, as I stand bereft
on Cemetery Lane amid oxeye daisies
   and columbine as thunder rumbles
in the mountains—
   she names me, words fall like rain,
slips among leaves, adds to streams—
   catches on wings just beginning to feather.

Where We Leave Our Name

Two rose buds this morning, worthy of an altar offering.
I place them in a blue vase, wonder if a name asks for stone

though I'm startled by this unlikely thought,
as though movement plays among leaves

or like the Flicker, feeding,
or the rainbow arching over marsh, scrim of earth's

rim. In the dead tree branch a Great Crested Flycatcher—
his gift of golden chest, his whistle, high-minded opera.

Sun stencils on my rose-patterned sofa pillows, sprightly,
as if to squelch my mood triggering, if not mirth, something akin.

I'm grateful for these interstices—hard lines and peek of flower.
What does it matter where I leave my name

or if our fingerprints vanish
or if we wind up dust mingled with water, great drops

in some ancient god's sea of mercy, my own inadequacy
no shock to a higher power.

Naming in the Garden at the Headwaters of the Tigris and the Euphrates

She may have been the first to say, *Garden,*
in ancient Hebrew or Arabic,
standing near a cedar of Lebanon,
pomegranate slipping from her tongue
in a pleasurable flow of syllables.

Did she spice the seasons with olives
or sabras or hearts of palm?
Did she slip through the garden among
Tamarisk trees and thornless vines,
watch the tiny wasp pollinate fig blossoms?

Perhaps she, mother of all of us, remembered
for tasting an apple—sauntered up to him,
who came first with her offering,
with knowledge: the only possible escape
from the gathering bramble was through desire.

Perseus' Dream

Once I watched Medusa trim her locks:
they fell about my feet
shorn edges slithering up my shins—

I whimpered as though I would be turned to stone.
One morning I dared to pull them one by one 'til
I could walk without the smell of death

though for days I worried   as I watched oyster shells
pile along the shore   white as skeletons abandoned
the way a man can leave his wife   or a woman her child.

I collected alabaster snail shells   cast-off feathers   shards
sharp as the off-shore wind—and smooth flat stones everywhere
cast by some gambling hand. How I wanted their dark gleaming:

the breath they whispered
the wings of their words.

Frog

Old and crusted with dirt,
    your skin a shade of olive so dark,

I fear my spade will mistake you
    for earth in need of turning.

Frog, slow to leap to safety
    from winter's cold blowing—

nothing blooming, though snowdrops
    made a promise they couldn't keep,

green stalks droop in defeat—
    warty frog, sing your horny song.

On this cracked lip of winter
    I await light, redeeming rain.

Words

newts hiding near the pond—ravel of thought breeding names: what are we to do with how they knife? Charming at times, an evanescent cascade like morning sun bordering moss: iridescent lace. In the mind, then gone—what was it? They give us algae, barnacles, humpbacks, conch, oyster catcher, crab. And like the neap tide, a least difference. Bone-blurred, moon, stars, marrow. Larva, juvenile, eft and adult. Fling them, let them shed. String them like chinaberries until you can wear them, make them your own.

The Narrow Shore

Where did it go, the once expanse, the stretch
   from dunes to the high-tide mark now so slight

      you step off the wooden walkway into lapping water.

Where is the star's light? the ancient splash
   of ruin, a wild ride in summer lost to quick tick of time.

      I ask you, what will we do in the late season

when the tide turns toward winter, and memories
   of old wading pools left by outgoing tide where

      sea biscuits, whelks, starfish and sand dollars cluster?

What's washed in wind? Girls lined in a row for photographs
   shadows pooling at feet on the rutted beach, their tenderness

      a left-behind heartache.

Je Ne Sais Quoi

Waccamaw Bridge, November

Blackbirds flock around me
so low I might touch a wing,
stretch my hand
out the car window
into their swarming darkness,
so willful in flight, these harbingers,
headed to roost
as evening parses each tree's leaves
into a vibrant shimmer,
I have come through eons
for this moment, this—
I don't know what—
flick of wing? Unspeakable joy?

Fog

Sunlight floods fog, blind drive over
        the Waccamaw
        crepuscular
        shadows slow me.

Trees in the marsh filter phantom
        shades. I steer by
        instinct, follow

flickering taillights of those I
        hope are less blind.
        We emerge in
        suffused luster,

pine trees escape the low-lying
        nebula. I
        lament the veil-
        imbued instant—

lost as though I had hung by my
        fingertips on
        earth's rim, drenched in

dream, released from the driven world—

Down to the Salt Meadow and Heaving Sea

Through every crevice and mountain vein of strata
rich with muted color, beauty welcomes,
as water and wind break whole rocks into sediment,

a metamorphosis so slow my fast-forward mind
flies past, unseeing, though I note their lofty reach.
My Grandfather, I remember, cupped his palms,

held then released the Word, as though
falcons circling blunted tops and bald knobs
though weary, weathered eons,

pummeling their steepness down to navigable paths
bordered by hellebore following foothills
through long meadows shimmering

with Queen Anne's lace and blazing star,
down to the salt meadow and heaving sea—
habitat of ox-eye, cord grass, and pluff mud—

where tides rise and fall for pleasure
casting the bay's sloshing waters
as if to slake some enormous thirst.

In the Blue Ridge Mountains

A phantom love creeping
      like smoke into my lungs—
            the way haze slips over mountains

You claw through memory as you
      must track in Africa, or India,
            deadly at times, your footfall on the path,

you behind me, my scent as though
      a kiss, imprinted on you, no matter
            how I lost myself in Stevens's

holy hush of ancient sacrifice ravishing
      earthly woods of words, while he
            remembers the boughs of summer—

you never lose my odor, prey that I am,
      I turn to close the distance—
            'til your growling, like a sleepy yawn,

pauses my advance toward
      a paring unlikely as a lamb to lay by you—
            We rise in the brisk morning's blue fog,

I drink coffee; you sip from unsullied stream
      We are never far from each other
            in tandem, always.

II

Absence Gathers

veils the oak, fills the street, fogs the hollow—

and lies between two newly planted crepe myrtles:

rain—no green grass on the red dirt. Sense it,

absence, watch it fold as a seamstress might gather

netted fabric or patterned silk in her capable hands.

After Your funeral

I found the one you kept
        in your wallet, it aged with you, sepia
                and creased.

I smile for you as I peel potatoes
        surrounded by wedding gifts,
                including two pitchers: one new,

the other my grandmother's blue willow,
        broken when our first child grabbed
                the table—

We were both more beautiful than I knew,
        uprooting ourselves to grow a home,
                though, of course, the photo doesn't show

the tangled love and anger a marriage makes—
        lessons in forgiveness of—your waking me
                with a gift, a quilt stitched square by seemingly

random square, as the maker
        cut and sewed, matching what couldn't be matched
                with lesser skill, patchwork merging

into a brilliant whole reminiscent of how we took
        years to shape patterns, sometimes a circle
                within a square, or dark fabric under

colored stars as though tender mercies shown
        through, our discretionary power to pardon
                kept together by stitches.

The Transient Nature of Things

Caught by a leveret at play in the meadow,
I put down the morning news, watch
bunny-leaps over clover in the still

wet morning. Nothing moves
except a twitching ear or his nibbling chin,
as he munches fresh Johnny-jump-ups.

Tomorrow he'll have vanished,
having scented my neighbor's bounding lab,

cheerful and sweet—as my friends describe me—
though I a stranger to this nature others see,

at times too weary to ferry my child
to the library, where she might discover
a word, a story, or a poem.

While I have all of eternity to sleep,
I savor my afternoon naps,
and this leaping young rabbit

at play in the meadow, not yet troubled
by hounds, though absence hovers over all.

As if I Blinked

Here—then not, reduced
to a few shutter clicks.

After all the years of being,
you're nothing I can see,

as if you slipped
from my passenger seat

into sudden mist,
a wisp in fog, gone—

your I-don't-give-a-damn glance,
eyes cut toward me,

your wry beauty lost—
the veil

lifted to reveal shade,
then no trace,

as if I blinked,
as if I wasn't watching

and missed the *Jesus Saves* sign
on the old barn near the highway—

Sign Language

Give me a sign—
a tap on the shoulder
a brush of wind against my cheek,
a movement—to or from—
in my periphery, my name whispered

Only me in this house, looking out,
I could swear you're there, edging the front yard,
planting Lenten roses—Will I have to live
no longer building on our thirty-nine years?

I am not in charge this dark morning,
as I try to let go, my heart knows nothing,
and the brain—erratic, disordered thoughts
elide into memory—not quick or caring,
and I, loose as an untied knot, hear no trace,
what's left of me following a strand
lost in nowhere—

We find ourselves

in what memory allows us, how we live
our myths—grandfather, whose work yields
sustenance, plows his Biblical field, farmers

and their wives wait for Preacher King's message.
Mother recites axioms like commandments:
A good name is rather to be chosen than great

riches when I lied about the glass. *The baby*
might put them in her mouth, she admonished.
I buried them, the polished glass shards,

I lamented their sunrise hues, creamy white
like rose quartz pink, gone to earth,
guarded by the clump of black rush

in the bleached oyster shell midden,
where I watched the swallow-tailed kite fly over,
like divine comfort—then the bird's shadow:

the V of its tail a message written on a cloud's white
page—wing-spangled memory, balanced at the river's
edge, my love for glass colors, and not my sister.
Not a trifle, to meet my greedier self.

Transubstantiation

Finality, how I hate every version of the word—
his final days, her finite life, death's finality.

      If I empty myself of will,
      will my soul give me peace?

I saw the beauty in our daily routine, never shook
my fist at you, though times were trying.

      I thought we were easy with one another.
      Were my prayers false? I believed

in the Mystical Body of Christ.
Of my faith, ask Saint Theresa for what that means.

      Thomas had the right idea. You were lovely
      in your silence, and I waiting, so needy.

Like Wings

Sprinting over un-furrowed rows,
thick with old field toad flax—
a doe bounds
through air, sun bright
on her taut brown coat,
legs elongated like wings,
as she leaps over the road
in front of my speeding car,
so close I see life in her eye—
awed by beauty's black flint,
tawny in her breeding velvet,
her sure, elegant leap at the exact second—
my held breath released, accepts this blessing.

Violets

I have tried to collect their corn-blue frailty
near the fence into clusters of sweet beguile—
why they resist, I do not know,
growing here and there as they do—
It is my garden, my will they are up against—
even the concrete patio cannot hold them
from edging through a crack:
>   from under the back steps, they peer—
>   refuse to flower, prefer to wrangle
>   thick groves of chickweed, dare me
>   to rank them with roses, so willing
>   to stay where I place them.

Snow in the Low Country

Wind whirls handfuls through trees—
not like children throwing snowballs,
but some playful *jeté,* a *coryphée*
dancing among piles of lingering white.

Weighted oaks sigh, green leaves shiver,
magnolia cones freeze but cling, flakes drift
as if an ice queen ladles dust over a blue-trimmed
cabin, staging it in vanilla crystals.

In the nearby marsh, cord grass stands sentinel,
yet sun's measure will melt flakes into pluff mud—
The snowflakes' intricate precision in falling,
a story told of flowing patterns, memory

a production in grace where theatre thrives,
though it fades, and the curtain falls too soon.

Bear

We are each other
we have one understanding
of the stars
    —N. Scott Momaday

What am I to make of your appearance in the clearing,
the forest's thick shadow smelling of moss, pine, lichen,
your fur the deep brown well I fall into, staring as you
rise on hind legs over me where I stand at wood's edge,
blinking into bright sun, then at you, like sudden lightning
rumbling from sky, paws scratching the air, mouth fierce
with all I do not know about myself.

Crows at My Feeder

They come to my feeder, though they prefer fields,
   carrion hidden among millet or yarrow, crows
with harsh calls in treetops and on empty beaches
   black feathers, velvet at the neck
dark eyes scavenging the wild—
   They light on the ground one after the other
as though dropped from a Chinaberry tree,
   its branches holding marble drupe, the fruit full
of memory, hard and sometimes poisonous—

You and me, our ear against the fence post,
   listen as the devil beats his wife in the sun-splashed
rain—we called the rain, made it fall in summer drops,
   prisms on the wings of crows amid rows of corn—
The bike ride down the hill, braking at the mud puddle
   straddling the road. You skidded, bike edging the ground,
water splashing in the skid. *Sister*, you yelled as though
   I could fling a net to enclose you—there the fence
the barbed-wire fence, like some medieval spiked torture tool
   digging into your arm, flesh torn away, fig fruit, blood red.
The inlet, daring you to jump alone in that brine, water
   an eddy of leaving, how I held my breath you, flailing about,
your mouth an obdurate pout. My hot words choked out
   I didn't mean it—

Crows again and wing flutter—
   think of wind's swirl, strewing leaves against damp lichen
clutching rocks, and now the crows at my feeder, wildly
   ravenous they will have the seeds before the Woodpecker,
the doves, the swifts and wrens. Dream of you in the flooded
   river, water coming over the bridge and I call the rain
trying to reach you as the crows in their patient
   flapping swoosh to shore—you
always against the tide.

Between the Rivers

sun flicks over widgeon grass, cattails white water lilies
      pine on the high ground, cypress and gum
            in the low places at soft shallow curves

of river's edge where wild rice grows near a tidal pool,
      where one might find wildness in geese scattering
            skyward quaking spatterdock as though to

bring forth sign from brackish, salt or fresh water,
      as though to unearth from muck a shimmer of oasis
            a sweating back at work on dikes, a tremulous

image near the shore of a two-mast yawl rowing North
      toward a boat casting off in heat waves
      safe passage

under skys atavistic yawn
      tribal spell already upon him
            ancestors on another shore, waiting.

On Waking with Anxiety

The Pacific could belch up a tsunami
   churned from the sea's floor

a roar of sucking air pulls water back
   as it meets shore—

you could be caught unaware
   by this wave on its way

to pound a village to bits
   you rowing frantically away from it

worse than my ten-year-old
   self trying to run from the mad dog

when he dug his teeth into my heel,
   followed by three weeks of daily shots

in my stomach, the twenty-first
   the only time I cried—

but clearly, we don't have a tsunami today,
   even the bay is calm, a boat sails

leisurely on the inland waterway—
   relax, eat a hamburger at the Marina,

bow to ineluctable fate,
   ask what you will of sea.

Grief Released

ebb tide eliding the once was—
                a life vanished.
back and forth the foam-covered brine,
                    scatters every
fragmented shell once collected:
                scallops, mussels—
                one like a wing
                in wind's hard spray.
It flings away this broken thing
                to ravel in
                a laughing gull's
                unruly bray.

III

Nothing to it,

forgetting yesterday:
I blow it like kisses to past phantoms
what could it want from me?
I close my eyes and squeeze my lips
to what comes creeping in a moment's
lapsed contemplation—
I won't take back all that burned
swiftly as paper—let the flame shimmer
               unshackled, a dalliance, nothing more.

And when the forest of your bearable life appears

after Katie Ford

Rising and unfolding, like a great beast
       or mangrove, no, a bamboo grove:

thick canes you'll need a machete
to navigate—imagine the strength you'll need
to hack a path through mature growth, cutting
away as if each cane's node could release
untold stories—

       Look up from your scything to wipe your brow—
       a boat idles among bald cypress,
       stacked with charts mapping the waterway,

              sun lighting an open seat—
              as if all you had to do was step aboard.

Geography

Sliver moon at 6 a.m., stars flung across the dark sky,
the big dipper ready to pour the day for you, old crone,
     to cradle the hours.

Orion is tired of chasing the Sisters.

Later in the morning, a dark flat base
of cumulus clouds twists down to the waters
     strong enough to push a boat away.

Across all our seas, tribes howling.

Rain bearing down on Gulf waters, waves whip
to shore, spent blossom strips away from the clustered
     fronds of the un-branched Sable Palmetto.

What's to be done?

Sun, coruscate of movement, a dance on water,
boats cutting through—out to fish,
     ignoring dark clouds off shore.

And other Gulfs?

Where is their moon, their stars,
their old crones to cradle
their blistered, swelling hours?

Easing Westward

A storm's first wind-driven waves keen
deep within the coastal trough.

I can stand on shore for only so long
amidst such howling dusk—

even a sandpiper, graceful on one foot,
head tucked under sheltering wing, retreats.

First light reveals a wrack of pungent seaweed,
broken shells and stones from the depths,
flung by some god's petulant offspring.

Secrets lie exposed in low tide—
an eagle's fletched head arrows toward prey.

Morning sheds dreamy residue, slathering
wheat-colored cord grass with gold.

Come forth, morning, with your wild pink sky.
Even if your light dims, easing westward
growing dreary with fresh overcast—

I remain fierce in my waiting.

From East Coast to West

The flight approaches Seattle, you abandon
the crossword puzzle and look up—shock of Mt. Rainer,
though you knew it was there.
The ferry from Victoria. You crossing Juan De Fuca
to Port Angeles. Stunningly clear day. Still there, Rainer.
You could offer yourself to that volcano.

Back home flour spills while you bake banana bread—
nuts, flung by the cutting knife, on your kitchen floor.
Out the window a painted bunting—
first of the season—scarlet breast,
indigo head, yellow-green mantle,
maybe immature, perched at the feeder.

And you think of Mt. Rainier,
so far away from your Atlantic coast
where hummingbirds, those tiny wings,
hum near your morning glory vine,
nothing and everything flaring
in your head, effulgent, unbent.

Wayfarers at Pearson's Falls

We watch the quicksilver shower break over rock, light
refracted by water as if to highlight how descent doesn't
end. We hold to our rock, crusted with lichen, kinship—
looking up the tumbled wet steps with wayfarers'
yearning, as if stairs leading to some bright world we
might approach, as if beckoned to enter.

Transmigration

Only the least sandpiper stayed to catch my thoughts,
birds themselves, flits of movement.

In Syria, the people are migrating
without compass, Bedouins without tents.

I feel the weight of the world, not free
like the Great White Pelican, sure of its route.

Endangered birds, the lesser kestrel, unable
to follow the fixed path to feed near waters.

In the trees next door, berries grow
up the trunk of a pine tree, into the branches,

like a musical score, lilting tempo
against the burl—a pouring out—

say the soul passing into the ethereal,
the lost feeding places, the blind going.

Grief Works Its Way

Grief hounds me, laps at my feet,
      sniffs over my sleep—not like a pet,
          but more like Cerberus.

Even the trees are lonely. It is the day of all souls—
      restless movement, and wandering—
          the night of rising sleepers.

Are the dead like silkworms cocooned in skin,
      waiting to break free of all earthly diversions
          as St. Theresa imagined?

All I know is this hand on my kitchen table,
      as I work the splinter from it,
          a tenderness for my old self—

a new person emerging from this hard case,
      a chrysalis with one wing out, trembling.

Tapestry

Snow dusts cedars, coats the fence,
the ripening quince and forsythia
threatens to quench their pink and yellow blooms—
snow and sun forge this morning mist,
ending the year of your brother's death,
warp and woof spins away
from those dun threads, lush green
crowns the light-splashed tree,
leaves bud under sky,
sing as your hands move over the loom,
threads crossing, then cross-hatching in tune.

Sister

She rises on this November morning
    in the dim shadowshine—
        yokes her horses to her wagon

her flint struck in the distance
    a flicker you think will go out
        but it gains the night

her light—how to name it—
    Garnet from out of nowhere
        violet-tinged mantle, streak of orange

coming on behind the mangroves
    the Chinese Tallow—she means her own glory
        her deep color furls upward—coming on

comes on, the chairmaker's rush lifting in greeting
    some red-winged blackbird whistles
        as she comes from the bottom of the sea

or maybe from her island in the West
    there—her eastern flare, the brother
        a full burn, breaking churn of light

Among Stones

Still as stone, by the riverbank
overlooking shimmering water,

you see two wolves streak across the meadow,
gray fur rippling in wind,

golden-rimmed irises focused on the path ahead—
through brambles of yellow stones and sagebrush.

Steam's hot hiss, now a frozen rush, mud pots
and geysers, volcanic breccias scattered like giant seeds.

Even a crusted river, hard as dolerite thaws
and courses in spring, but you only hear loss—

give it up, your frozen riverbed, you are in some lost place
stuck, away from lambent light, when all around you

snow melts, creatures howl, nature rumbles—
wade upriver, even if you have to break the ice.

While Drinking Coffee & Eating Apricot Preserves

I felt my book of days turn as a red-shouldered hawk
settled in leafless branches of a cherry blossom tree—

I sipped my coffee's dark scent, my mouth savoring chicory,
its thick sweet-wanting, while hawk spun his head

as owl might, from front to back, searching as I
dipped my finger in the apricot preserves,

remembered my bird book, and how I sighted
a painted bunting on the day my aunt died—

then hawk spread his wings-attire in his heavy
lift-off, enchantment so lightly rising into the air

the swift of it a breath-catch as though a feather
brushed my cheek, the weighty send-up of soul,
a melody of nimble wind, light's path, soaring—

What I Don't Begrudge

The way leaves bud or falling acorns fill October,
or a squirrel's deliberation hoarding the bitter meat
I hope tastes sweet to her in winter.

See how she darts, settles on her haunches,
a nut in her dexterous claw like a shopper
checking Brussels sprouts for freshness.

I've lost count of the miles away from past selves
sculling lost seas—I am who I've come to be—
at times reckless or unaware, or unmovable

preferring silent meditation in morning,
sometimes preceded by my groaning,
lowing day like some balky loaded truck.

In my 80th year, I watch the moon rise
and set each day, a blessing—trust its orbit,
its faithful fullness and diminishing phases.

Trust each day's chiaroscuro, each moment,
opening like a crocus and when blooms are spent,
lying fallow, gathering strength for what comes next.

I turn the soil to clip each wilted blossom,
and mulch the thirsty branching roots—
gardener, caretaker for spring and summer blooms.

A Shim in Quaking Water

throat pulsed with song, unlike the blue birds in my blue bowl on my heart pine coffee table—hushed bluebirds flying into blue branches of welcoming blue trees. And the three sunflowers in a purple vase keep memories of what the sun was like, how petals scattered in a hot wind, their swoosh distant as a moody song. I listen, uncertain—I miss so many people, but only whitecaps hear their clearly spoken language—I remember how light skimmed a moonbow over the sea's surface while Saturn, Mars, Venus, queued up in the starlight distance, away from what I can know. I saw the colors, a shim in the quaking water. I found petals in my blue bowl and my morning warbler sings loud enough for me to hear.

Metamorphosis

Take my cremains to a field of sunflowers,

on a day when rain refreshes the parched,

    extravagant heads, reverently bent

        for a moment of ceremony,

    sowing my ashes like seeds,

    as rain moistens to a gritty puddle

        where beauty roots.

I want to have counted as something fertile,

to have birthed something,

even one flower, in the universe.

Morning Glory

Amethyst freeloader takes
bold possession of my garden
brags over a concrete post
as if it were a podium
path assured until sun's hot
breath bears upon the bloom
folding the flower
into a soundless trumpet
leaning into its light
blowing a brief note
        an ovule of embryo
        a stone ripe for sowing.

Notes

"Meteor Shower" italicized line from Walt Whitman's "As I Ebb'd with the Ocean of Life."

"Consider the Cardinal" was inspired by T. S. Eliot's, "Journey of the Magi."

"She Who Listens to Hummingbirds" was written for Joy Harjo and in memory of my grandmother.

"In the Blue Ridge Mountains" italicized lines are from Wallace Stevens' "Sunday Morning."

"After your funeral" was written in memory of my husband, John Bernardin, Sr., through thirty-nine years my most ardent supporter.

"And when the forest of your bearable life appears" is a line from Katie Ford's, "The Fire," from her book *Blood Lyrics*.

"A Letter to Susan in Ireland" italicized lines from Seamus Heaney's "Digging" and "The Haw Lantern."

Acknowledgments

There are moments in our writing lives, ringing with astonishment, that we thought to take a particular workshop or make a new friend. Joy Harjo's workshop of many years ago is one such moment. Joy gave me the courage to step forward, to trust my voice and to speak from the heart. Her workshop participants and the Aspen Writers' Conference gave much support.

The phenomenal writing group we called the Deadline Club edged me toward more reading of other poets and provided sharp comments aimed at my sometimes-weak phrases and lines. You know who you are, and I still love you and miss you.

Another such moment came when I met the late Susan Laughter Meyers, or became a close friend, as I had met her years earlier. Susan read many poems, offered comments improving craft and clarity. She read this manuscript more than once. I am honored by her belief in my ability to sing. How I miss her voice.

Numerous poet/teachers have guided and inspired me. Two years attending the Palm Beach Poetry Festival studying with the lyrical Jane Hershfield and the inimitable Nick Flynn open my mind and heart to what I could do in poetry. Later, Laure Anne Bosselear read this manuscript and offered much encouragement.

Yet another moment came when poet and editor April Ossmann agreed to read my manuscript. She edited this manuscript with a sharp eye, offering comments, insight, and direction toward metaphor. Her willingness to keep with me as we progressed together through these poems is immeasurable. I am most grateful.

I am indebted to the Poetry Society of South Carolina, the North Carolina Poetry Society for awards and publication of my poems, and the South Carolina Arts Commission for a Literary Fellowship, a strong encouragement to pursue my work; and, to Kwame Dawes, who chose my chapbook, *The Book of Myth*, for the South Carolina Poetry Initiative, my first collection.

To Pat Riviere-Seel and John Lane for their attention to and comments on my poems. To Kevin Morgan Watson and Press 53 for selecting this book, a first full collection, and perhaps my most thrilling poetic moment when I read Kevin's email of acceptance.

Other poets who read individual poems and steered me toward clarity are Ann Herlong-Bodman, Susan Finch Stevens, Carol Peters, Rene Miles, and Curtis Derrick. Over the years, many friends and relatives, too numerous to mention, encouraged and supported my work.

Thanks to all my family, my children, and grandchildren who support me, and especially Phil Wilkinson, biologist, researcher, photographer, my partner, always.

Cover artist Phil Wilkinson is an internationally known wildlife biologist, author, and nature photographer. He was raised at Hopsewee Plantation on the North Santee River in Georgetown, South Carolina. His work as a field biologist has been awarded over the years, most recently for his publications on his nine-year study about alligators in and around the Santee Delta.

Photo by Philip Wilkinson

Libby Bernardin has published two chapbooks, *The Book of Myth* (SC Poetry Initiative, 2009) and *Layers of Song* (Finishing Line Press, 2011). Her poems have appeared in *Notre Dame Review*, *Asheville Poetry Review*, *Southern Poetry Review*, *Cairn*, *Kakalak*, *Pinesong*, and the Poetry Society of South Carolina *Yearbook*s. She is a Life Member of the Board of Governors of the South Carolina Academy of Authors, and a member of the Poetry Society of South Carolina and the North Carolina Poetry Society. Her poem "Transmigration" was nominated for a 2017 Pushcart Prize.

www.ingramcontent.com/pod-product-compliance
Lightning Source LLC
LaVergne TN
LVHW041345080426
835512LV00006B/616